Say it in writing

What every genius, dropout, scholar, writer, bureaucrat or just plain average Joe should know about writing for the ear.

Simple steps to making your writing

As smooth as silk!

Say it in writing

What every genius, dropout, scholar, writer, bureaucrat or just plain average Joe should know about writing for the ear.

Simple steps to making your writing

As smooth as silk!

Don Ray

Don Ray is a veteran, multi-media journalist, author and lecturer. He has written for scores of television station and radio outlets, newspapers and magazines. He has taught writing at California State University at Los Angeles, UCLA Extension and other schools. He's written or ghostwritten six books on investigations, interviewing, document interpretation and open sources of investigation.

Don Ray has won writing and producing awards for his work in television, radio and newspapers. And, he has trained thousands of journalists, law enforcement investigators, private investigators and genealogists in information gathering, interviewing and smooth writing.

If you have any questions or would like to book him as a teacher, trainer or lecturer, please contact him by email at donray@donray.com or contact Creative Continuum at (714) 524-9566.

ISBN 0-9713804-5-7

Published in the United States by

continuum
1213 Athens Avenue
Placentia, CA 92870
714-524-9566
www.creativecontinuum.com

Table of Contents

Introduction

One of the biggest failures of the education system in the United States is its absolute inability to teach people how to write in a manner that others can easily understand. The closest educators come is when kids are in elementary school. Youngsters have no difficulty writing clear, simple sentences that just about anyone can understand. There's a reason they take to writing so well – they write the way they speak. By the second or third grade, children have mastered the ability to speak the English language about as well as most adults have. And they write the way they speak – conversationally.

It's when children get into middle school and high school that the academia folks begin their relentless task of crushing that natural writing skill in each student. It's at that time the education system snatches away the well-written textbooks and replaces them with books written by educators *for* other educators. For the next five to ten years, the students must read some of the worst writing they'll experience in their lifetimes. They must struggle through painfully long sentences peppered with words they'll only use in their school careers. They'll read and reread passages that would require a surgeon to repair – passages laden with long, dependent clauses and difficult-to-understand terminology.

The students are trapped in an unreal world – almost like a

secret society with its own secret language. It's a world where nobody dares to be caught writing in the same, simple and natural way that we speak. Believe it or not, the high school dropouts often have the advantage. One of the best writers I ever encountered never completed the eight grade. I used his natural and dynamic writing to teach newspaper writers how to make their stories come alive. I'll admit that it felt strange explaining to professional writers that more people would read and enjoy their stories if they wrote in simple sentences using active verbs – where the doer of the action is the subject of the sentence and the recipient of the action follows as the object.

I'm talking about writing the way we speak. It should make sense to anyone that it's easier to read and understand things that are written exactly the way people talk. But no, that's too easy for the writers of textbooks. How can publishers of textbooks get away with charging students and school districts the outrageous prices they charge if the books aren't overflowing with academic jargon? And how can any self-respecting educator impress his or her colleagues if they write a book that's easy to read?

By the time the brighter students near graduation, they've learned to never get caught writing in a simple, speakable style. They've learned to turn every simple or compound sentence into a complex sentence by adding one or more dependent clauses to the beginning, the middle or the end. They've learned to replace just about every common, understandable word with ten-dollar words that impress their teachers but confound and confuse their readers. And the more their writing is filled with gobbledygook, the happier their teachers are.

Okay, I'm ranting and raving a bit here. I will concede that there are some brave, rebel educators out there who are trying to buck the old system. They're whispering behind closed classroom doors and closed blinds. They're telling kids it's okay to write the way they speak. But there's a good chance they're swearing these fortunate students to secrecy. And I'm sure they're telling these enlightened, natural writers to be ready at a moment's notice to revert to stilted writing the minute they encounter any of the traditional Writing Gestapos.

Those fortunate students who take the secret oath and break the outmoded rules are the ones who will end up being the great modern writers. They'll be the ones to make a fortune writing ad copy and television news scripts. They're the ones who will be rewarded for simplicity. It's *their* work that people will read and enjoy.

Foreword

This book is about writing in a more simple, easy-to-read manner – writing in relaxed style that will encourage people to continue to read. Your readers will probably not know exactly why they enjoy reading your stuff – they'll just want to read more. They may comment that you have a great writing style, but they won't know why. That's because your writing will be so natural. The readers won't be able to pinpoint your secret because it will be hidden in everyday language.

As you read and start practicing each writing tip in this book, you'll very quickly start noticing a difference in what you write as well as in what you read and even hear. You'll begin to notice that others are using this simple, but effective writing style. You'll quickly realize that the popular author you've been reading writes in active-voice sentences, uses common words and avoids lengthy dependent clauses. You'll see your new writing style in advertisements, on billboards and in the better magazines and newspapers. And you'll hear network television anchors and reporters as they read scripts someone wrote in this conversation style.

You'll also begin to listen to the way people talk. You'll realize that we speak mostly in active voice. We use simple or compound sentences instead of dependent-clause-ridden complex sentences. Our sentences are fairly short, and we're more likely to use common terms for things. Indeed, you'll hear more jargon, but you'll realize that good writers aren't afraid to use common jargon in their writing.

On the flip side, you'll start to see bad writing everywhere. It will show up in club or company newsletters, in letters to the editor and especially in business letters and memos. And you'll hear this convoluted language in local television ads and on local television news programs as well as in very low-budget documentaries.

I first noticed it when I'd stay home from school and my mother would write me an excuse. "Please excuse Don as he was ill with the flu." I realized she didn't talk that way. She was more likely to say to someone, "Don's got the flu," or "Don's sick today." She'd never use "as" that way when she spoke – she'd say "*because* he was sick." I figured that was the way we were supposed to write such stuff. And now I know that my mother was just another victim of school-induced gobbledygook.

By the time you've ventured most of the way through this book you'll catch yourself writing things you never dared writing before. You'll use contractions as often as you use them when you speak. You'll occasionally slip and write the word "utilize" and then quickly change it to "use." You'll begin to realize that you can cut out entire paragraphs and replace them with well-written sentences. You'll understand that less is almost always better – and almost always clearer to the reader.

Don't be surprised if you reject some of the suggestions I'm offering you. Everyone is different and everyone has their own speaking style. There are some people who don't want to be anything less than dignified in all walks of life. There are others who will use humor even in the most somber moments. I'm certain that you'll find your own comfort level and you'll start writing in your own, unique voice. That's cool.

One last note – don't even think I'm going to force-feed you all kinds of technical names for parts of speech. If you don't know what a gerund is now, you probably won't know one when you're done reading this book – you'll just won't be using them as much as other people. I'm going to assume you know that a noun is a person, place or thing and that a verb is an action word. You probably remember that an object is the recipient of the action and usually finds itself toward the end of a sentence – at least toward the end of a well-written sentence. I'll talk a lot about dependent clauses and about active and passive voice. Don't worry, you'll find that they're easy to understand and easy to deal with. More than anything, you'll start seeing those dratted dependent clauses everywhere and you may get sick when you see all of the trash that people write using passive voice.

The reason you don't need to know the names of all the parts of speech is that you already know how to speak them – and if you learn to write the way you speak, you won't have any problems.

Do me one last favor – please do not track down and begin stalking your ninth-grade English teacher. He or she did not know any better and only wanted to survive in education and not have the Word Gestapo lurking in the classroom and hoping to catch them writing the way common people speak.

Writing Tip Number One

Write in short, simple sentences

Avoid the urge to put all of your information in one sentence. Have faith that the reader will endure a period or two and continue reading. The typical victim of schools of bad writing feels compelled to begin sentences with dependent clauses or use them elsewhere in the sentences. Okay, here's your first definition. Again, I promise you you won't have to memorize a lot of stuff.

A dependent clause often lacks either a subject or a verb and must be hook up with a complete sentence to make any sense. It cannot stand on its own. Here are some examples of sentences that begin with dependent clauses:

While he was living in Chicago, he went to a lot of Cubs games at Wrigley Field.

Pursuant to an act of Congress, desert tortoises are considered an endangered species.

A gambler in his twenties, Randy made a mess of his life and ended up in debt most of the time.

After she had completed college and graduate school, Hillary began looking for a suitable career in advertising.

Born in England in 1899, Sebastian spent his early years putting up with a most abusive father and a jewel of a mother.

Loving his work from the day he started, Armstrong had perfect attendance and rarely took vacations.

Notice that the dependent clauses cannot stand on their own. If they were to stand alone, they wouldn't make any sense:

While he was living in Chicago.

Pursuant to an act of Congress.

A gambler in his twenties.

After she had completed college and graduate school.

Born in England in 1899.

Loving his work from the day he started.

They don't work because they're dependent upon a complete sentence. A complete sentence is not dependent upon another phrase – so it's an independent clause. The best way to eliminate the dependent clause is to make it a sentence of its own by adding the necessary subject or verb or by removing key words such as "while," "after" or "because." Here's how you'd fix them:

He lived in Chicago.

It was pursuant to an act of Congress.

He was a gambler in his twenties.

She had completed college and graduate school.

He was born in England in 1899.

He loved his work from the day he started.

If these don't feel right or sound right or seem to be what you want to say, you can change them another way – you can make them into dependent clauses and use a conjunction (a word that connects two independent sentences) and create a compound sentence:

He was living in Chicago, so he went to a lot of Cubs games at Wrigley Field.

It was an act of Congress that put desert tortoises on the endangered species list.

Randy was gambler in his twenties, and he made a mess of his life and ended up in debt most of the time.

Hillary completed college and graduate school and

then began looking for a suitable career in advertising.

Sebastian was born in England in 1899 and spent his early years putting up with a most abusive father and a jewel of a mother.

Armstrong loved his work from the day he started, and so he had perfect attendance and rarely took vacations.

We speak in simple and compound sentences, so people find it easier to read simple and compound sentences. Listen to people talk and you'll begin to hear strings of independent clauses strung together with conjunctions. You probably don't want to write with so many compound sentences, however:

"Yesterday we went to the race track and we bet on a lot of horses, but we lost most of our money because we bought the programs from the wrong guys because we had parked in a different parking lot and had to use a different entrance that had different vendors there."

Granted, it's not the most appealing sentence in the world, but I'll bet you would have easily understood it had you heard someone say it aloud. I guarantee you you wouldn't hear someone speaking the sentence the way many people would write it:

Having parked in a different parking lot which caused

us to use a different entrance, we bet on the wrong horses, losing a lot of money because of having to purchase programs from different guys from whom we normally buy them.

I think you'll agree the second version would be impossible to understand if someone spoke it. My point is that it's not at all easy to understand it if you're reading it.

Dependent clauses in the middle of a sentences can cause even more problems because they often separate the subject of the sentence from the verb or the verb from its object:

The foreman on the work crew, a man known to many as a hard-working, hard-drinking jack of all trades, had three small children.

The drive along the highway, which was built during the early years of the Depression by members of the Works Progress Administration, a federal jobs program, can be a pleasant one.

Three climbers, accompanied by their local guides and each carrying a supply of water, a radio and 85 pounds of other equipment, started their journey.

The truth is, despite what you may have heard from reports in the media or from gossip around the water cooler, no jobs are going to be eliminated.

The congregation donated, without any regard for their own savings or retirement plans, two thousand dollars.

These complex sentences are not incorrect – just clumsy. My theory is that the dependent clauses deserve the oomph of being sentences that can stand alone. Again, the way to make these more effective is to break them into separate sentences – make the dependent clauses complete sentences. See if these don't read better:

The foreman on the work crew was known to many as a hard-working, hard-drinking jack of all trades. He had three small children.

The drive along the highway can be a pleasant one. It was built during the early years of the Depression by members of the Works Progress Administration. The WPA was a federal jobs program.

Three climbers started their journey. They were accompanied by their local guides. Each carried a supply of water, a radio and 85 pounds of other equipment.

The truth is, no jobs are going to be eliminated. That's despite what you may have heard from reports in the media or from gossip around the water cooler.

The congregation donated two thousand dollars. Its members had no regard for their own savings or retirement plans.

And, of course, people also like to put dependent clauses at the ends of sentences:

The lake was filled to capacity for the first time, giving boaters and swimmers a chance to cool off during the hot summer months.

The copier repairman wrapped up the job two hours earlier than expected, which made the manager grin from ear to ear.

More than half of the revenue came from Girl Scout Cookies and magazine subscriptions, which enabled the girls to make the trip to Hawaii.

Neither of them thought they'd ever see each other again, so they spent the night together, resulting in the birth of their daughter, Melissa, nine months later.

Judy could not have been happier when she finally completed basic training and was able to come home, proving to her doubting Thomas father that she was, indeed, capable of completing something.

They're all acceptable sentences, but people could more easily read them if the sentences were simple or compound:

The lake was filled to capacity for the first time. It gave boaters and swimmers a chance to cool off during the hot summer months.

The copier repairman wrapped up the job two hours earlier than expected, and that made the manager grin from ear to ear.

More than half of the revenue came from Girl Scout Cookies and magazine subscriptions. It enabled the girls to make the trip to Hawaii.

Neither of them thought they'd ever see each other again, so they spent the night together. Nine months later, their daughter Melissa was born.

Judy could not have been happier when she finally completed basic training and was able to come home. She was finally able to prove to her doubting Thomas father that she was, indeed, capable of completing something.

One of the strongest arguments for eliminating most of the dependent clauses in your writing is that you will be giving the clauses the punch they deserve. Cooling off in the hot summer months deserves to be a sentence of its own. The fact that the manager grinned is important enough to be an independent clause. The trip to Hawaii is the point of the sentence. Why not let it stand alone? Certainly Melissa's birth should not seem like an afterthought – it, too, should be a separate sentence. And Judy's victory at home was the point of the whole sentence – why diminish it by making it a dependent clause?

Here's a simple rule of thumb: If you feel the need to insert a coma in your sentence, you've probably written a dependent clause. Try to put a period or a conjunction where the comma was and see if it works better as two sentences. Of course, you may have to alter the dependent clause to make it a complete sentence.

A final note – don't infer from my short-sentence tirade that an occasional longer sentence is taboo. When you use compound sentences – and the two independent clauses relate to each other, a longer sentence is fine. It's the long sentences with the dependent clauses that force the reader to work harder.

Exercise Number One

Eliminate all of the dependent clauses in the sentences below by creating simple or compound sentences:

The Titanic, which was touted as being completely safe and unsinkable, collided with an iceberg in the North Atlantic and ended up on the ocean floor.

Having contracted polio when he was a child, Matthew never developed the motor skills that were required of a welder on skyscrapers.

Anna knew the combination to the safe, but she didn't want anyone to ever accuse her of stealing something, which is exactly what happened on that fateful Friday in September.

The grandchildren, ranging in age from six months to 23 years, had never been under the same roof before.

Unable to swim in rough current, Michael grew more and more fatigued, eventually causing him to give up hope completely.

Writing Tip Number Two

Use words and terms everyday people use.

Don't buy into the belief that people will think you're more sophisticated in you use bigger or more complicated words. I think the opposite is true – I think you come off looking like an arrogant person trying to be a know-it-all.

It's easy to fall into the big word trap when you read what others have written. I always get a kick out of reading letters average people write to lawyers or about legal issues. They've heard the phrases on TV or read them in documents. Instead of writing, "I wish to file a complaint against Apricot Bumfish," they'll write, "I wish to register a complaint against *one* Apricot Bumfish."

Here are some examples of sentences that include words or expressions that you should be able to simplify.

The tanker was filled with approximately 20 million gallons of crude oil and 25 personnel.

The vehicle containing six individuals, three of them were males, did not halt its forward progress at the electronic traffic device.

The aircraft made four revolutions around the airport in order to deplete its supply of fuel.

The man approached the edifice on foot, lingered near the door and then exited the area and repeated the actions in close proximity to the adjacent edifice.

The young mother perambulated her daughter along the thoroughfare and passing motorists observed her provocative apparel.

They're all correct sentences, but I think you'll agree this is not the way the average person speaks – as least if they want to have friends in their lives. There are a lot of ways to make these more speakable and more readable. Here's how I would do them:

The tanker was filled with about 20 million gallons of crude oil and had a crew of 25.

The car with six people inside – three of them men – ran the red light.

The pilot circled the airport four times to use up the plane's fuel.

The man walked up the building, stood by the door and then walked over to the building next door and did the same thing.

The young mother in a sexy outfit pushed her stroller down the street and caught the eye of people driving by.

Exercise Number Two

Look for words, terms or expressions in the following sentences that you might be able to replace with more common words:

The two adolescents spent the evening imbibing and then regurgitating.

The man demonstrated extreme paternalistic tendencies when he engaged in discourse with the young man.

The candidate for the position demonstrated a measurable deficiency when it came to a history of related employment.

She had exceeded her level of tolerance for coping with the behaviors of overactive fifth graders.

Whenever there was a periodic lowering of the conversation level, the professor opined as to the derivation of the current trends in fashion.

He was more than satisfactorily ensconced in his chair and refused to extricate himself when a member of the female persuasion approached the immediate area.

The octogenarian was 100 percent incapable of determining the location of his walking aid and consumed himself in humiliating self guilt when he was informed that he had hung it on the doorknob.

Writing Tip Number Three

Write in the active voice.

If you learn nothing else from this book, you should learn to recognize sentences that are in the passive voice. If you can't recognize them, you can't repair them. And the best way to repair them is to convert them to the active voice.

Here are two simple definitions:

Active voice – an active sentence is one in which the doer of the action is the subject of the sentence. If there's a recipient of the action, it is the direct object, and it will follow the verb.

Example – "Barbara ate the entire cake. Notice that the doer of the action is "Barbara," the action word is "ate" and the recipient of the action, "the cake," follows as the direct object.

Passive voice – a passive sentence is one in which the recipient of the action is the subject of the sentence. A helping verb – always a form of the verb "to be" – comes next, right in front of a verb in the past tense. The doer of the action may not even appear in the passive voice sentence. If it does, it will always follow the verb as the direct object.

Example – "The entire cake was eaten by Barbara," or simply, "The entire cake was eaten."

Notice that the cake is the recipient of action – it was eaten (*was* is the helping verb here). And notice that we have the option of not even identifying the person doing the eating. That's what makes passive-voice sentences the favorite of so many people. And that's why it's such a plague to good writing.

A passive sentence allows the doer of the action to remain secret – or at least to quietly hide at the end of the sentence. Bureaucrats especially love passive-voice sentences because it enables them to not have to take responsibility for their actions. Watch how cleverly people can escape responsibility in the following passive-voice sentences:

It has been decided you will be working the graveyard shift.

The vacation has been shortened from two weeks to one week.

Your application has been denied.

Your grandson has been shot and killed.

Your car has been repossessed.

If you continue speaking, you will be asked to leave the room.

You will be arrested and you may be convicted of a

crime and sent to jail.

The money was confiscated and the man was fired.

The bribe has been paid.

An apology will be made.

If you weren't paying attention as you read these typically vague and bureaucratic sentences, please read them again. Notice that, in every case, the subject of the sentence is the recipient of the action. And notice that a helping verb precedes each verb. And notice that the writer has oh-so-cleverly avoided identifying the doer of the action – the person or persons responsible for the action.

These are passive-voice sentences. And if we were to add the doer of the action to each sentence, we'd still have passive-voice sentences. Watch:

It has been decided *by me* that you will be working the graveyard shift.

The vacation has been shortened *by your supervisor* from two weeks to one week.

Your application has been denied *by me*.

Your grandson has been shot and killed *by one of our officers.*

Your car has been repossessed *by us.*

If you continue speaking, you will be asked *by me* to leave the room.

You will be arrested *by our security guard* and you may be convicted *by a judge or jury* of a crime and sent *by a judge* to jail.

The money was confiscated *by the comptroller* and the man was fired *by his supervisor.*

The bribe has been paid *by me.*

An apology will be made *by me.*

Notice that the sentences are still passive and they don't sound good. You should also notice that sometimes the doer of the action is not at the end of the sentence, but rather in the middle of the sentence – right after the verb. As awkward as these sentences seem, the writer has placed the doers of the actions in their proper places. And, I repeat, they are all still passive voice sentences.

Let's take a look at how these sentence would read in the active voice:

I decided you will be working the graveyard shift.

Your supervisor shortened your vacation from two

weeks to one week.

I denied your application.

One of our officers shot your grandson.

We repossessed your car.

If you continue speaking, I will ask you to leave the room.

Our security guard will arrest you, a judge or jury may convict you of a crime and a judge may send you to jail.

The comptroller confiscated the money and the man's supervisor fired him.

I paid the bribe.

I will apologize.

Wouldn't it be wonderful if people in power would be so honest and up front? As long as there are passive-voice sentences, however, they'll continue to be written (Oops, I just wrote a passive-voice sentence. Okay, I'll do it right). As long as there are passive-voice sentences, those damn bureaucrats will continue to write them. So there!

Aside from being boring sentences that sometimes allow the doer of the action to remain anonymous, passive voice sentences can confuse the writer and result in some humorous errors. Read the following sentences:

The body of a North Hollywood woman was found stuffed in the back of her car.

The cause of death was determined to be strangulation.

As you can see, they're both passive-voice sentences. And you'll note that we don't have a clue as to who the doers of the actions were. Well, when the newspaper reporter wrote these two sentences, he did identify some of the doers of the action. Read the following sentences as the reporter actually wrote them and you should be able to detect a couple of problems:

The body of a North Hollywood woman was found stuffed in the back of her car by police.

The cause of death was determined to be strangulation by the coroner.

Does it shock you at all that the coroner strangled the poor woman and then the police stuffed her body in the back of her car? That's what the reporter wrote.

As you can see, it's very easy to put the doer of the action in the wrong place in a passive sentence – and inadvertently cause it to modify the wrong phrase. To be correct passive-voice sentences the reporter should have written:

> The body of a North Hollywood woman was found *by police* stuffed in the back of her car.

> The cause of death was determined *by the coroner* to be strangulation.

By now you should be starting to see the structure of passive-voice sentences. And maybe you're even seeing how to convert them to the active voice.

> The police found the body of a North Hollywood woman after someone stuffed it in the back of her car.

> The coroner determined that the cause of death was strangulation.

Did you notice in the first sentence that it's possible to make it active even if we don't know who stuffed the body? It's reasonable to assume that a person stuffed the woman's body in the back of the car. We don't know who stuffed it, but we know it had to be somebody. Somebody did it. Active voice.

By now, you should be able to recognize the difference between and passive-voice sentence and an active-voice sentence.

Eventually, you'll find yourself writing most everything in the active voice. But until then, you might want to check your work and use this simple formula for converting passive to active voice:

1. Look for the verb — the action word. If there's a helping verb in front of it — "is," "was," "has been," "will be," "had been," "would have been," "will have been," etc. — and the verb seems to be in the past tense, you're probably looking at a passive-voice sentence.

2. When you've identified the verb, ask yourself "Who is the doer of this action?" Remember, in a passive voice sentence, it may be the direct object or it may not exist at all. You must determine who the doer of the action is.

3. Rewrite the sentence using the doer of the action as the subject of the sentence. You will not need the helping verb and the new form of the verb you use may not need to be in the past tense.

4. Check your sentence again to make sure that the doer of the action is the subject, the verb stands alone and the recipient of the action (if there is one) is the direct object.

5. Be sure to read the entire sentence to make sure there are no other passive-voice phrases in your new sentence.

Once you've written your sentence in the active voice you'll be able to look at your verb and see if you can replace it with a more powerful, descriptive or punchy verb. You'll learn that in Writing Tip Number Four. But first, another exercise.

Exercise Number Three

Identify any passive-voice sentences below and change them to active-voice sentences. If you can't identify the doer of the action, take a guess or use "somebody" or "someone." And remember, you may be looking at a sentence that is already active. Keep in mind, it's possible to use a form of the verb "to be" in situations where the sentence is active.

The decision was made following four hours of deliberation by the jury.

I would have been promoted if my resume would have been looked at.

The window was broken by the rock that was kicked up by the wheels of the truck.

The problem was one of the biggest problems Stephen had ever encountered.

The rental car was driven hard and returned in horrible shape.

It was clear that the soldiers would not return in time to rescue the women.

The diamond was sold to the woman at a 50-percent discount.

The man was shot by the wishing well.

The suspect was given the opportunity by the police to make one phone call.

The work was not done the way it should have been done.

Dinner was prepared by the great aunt and her six nieces and was served by the great nieces.

The football was kicked clear over the goal post and clear out of the stadium.

The payments were made on time in most cases, but was delayed when the roads were covered with snow in the winter.

It has been brought to my attention that you have been assaulted in the past.

She was happy her son was finally coming home from the long vacation.

It has been pointed out that the man was never as happy as he was when he was a living in Stockton.

Writing Tip Number Four

Make your verbs come alive.

Back when you were writing in passive voice, you pretty much had no way of doing much about the verb. But when you make the sentence an active-voice sentence, you have the freedom to decide if you could be using a different, more descriptive, more powerful verb.

Many would-be creative writers make the mistake of depending upon descriptive words – adjectives and adverbs – to add color, depth, meaning and maybe even excitement to their writing. Indeed, there are places for these modifiers, but when a writer overuses them, the writing suffers. Here's a "for instance:"

"She proudly walked past the envious, judgmental crowd without hearing their cruel and demeaning statements."

There's certainly nothing incorrect about the sentence, but you'll notice that all of the description comes from adverbs (proudly) and adjectives (envious, judgmental, cruel and demeaning). If I didn't point this out to you, you probably wouldn't have noticed that the verbs are as stale as last week's popcorn – "walked" and "hearing."

The verbs are what make a scene come to life. What if the writer had the woman "parading" past the people? Or maybe "strutting?" And is there a better way of showing the reader what the crowd was doing. In this case, the writer told you what they were doing – he didn't show you. Did they jeer her? Did they belittle her? Did they demean her? Maybe they blasted her with raspberries. And did the woman not hear them or did she ignore them? Maybe she shut them out. Maybe she pretended to not hear. There are so many possibilities when you decide to make the verbs come alive.

"A gunshot was heard."

Hey, did you notice right away the passive voice sentence? Make the sentence active and you can describe the event from various places in the scenario.

"Something exploded outside the door and instantly Emily gasped and clutched her pearl necklace."

"The shock wave of the exploding gun powder bounced off the wall, rattled the china and then converged on Emily's entire nervous system. She sprang to her feet and then dove for the floor."

It's all in the verbs. How about this one:

"The incredibly experienced scoutmaster carefully and skillfully started the fire."

Did you notice the adjective (experienced) and the adverbs (incredibly, carefully and skillfully)? What's the verb? It's "started." Let's try to show *how* the scoutmaster started the fire rather than telling the reader *that* he did it.

"The scoutmaster peeled the bark off the kindling wood and wove in the newspaper he had torn into strips. He whipped his right hand along the thigh of his dungarees and beamed as the wooden match burst into flame..."

You'll begin seeing passive-voice sentences everywhere you look, but you'll have to really work at watching the verbs. Remember, modifiers tell the reader what something looks like or how something moves — verbs show the action.

Exercise Number Four

Bring the verbs in the following sentences to life:

The secretary angrily left the office.

The rosebud opened up to become a beautiful, red rose.

Earl tried and tried to remember the name of his high school teacher.

The giant wave came to shore and hit the restaurant so hard there was nothing left afterwards.

The real estate agent said he was astoundingly angry as he shouted at the customer.

The highway patrolman cautiously walked up to the passenger's side of the van he had just pulled over.

The trail went from the bottom of the Grand Canyon to the top.

Writing Tip Number Five

Lighten up and have some fun.

One of the best feature writers I know is Pat Murkland. She's been writing for the Riverside Press-Telegram for years. When you read her stories, you can tell she enjoys the work – she has fun. The best tip she ever gave me was, "Every so often, give your readers a gift of some kind."

The gifts she gives seem to come every three or four paragraphs. It may be a quote that makes you chuckle, or a description of something that seems to come out of left field – but works, or a clever way of saying something or an anecdote that makes you shake your head. I recall one story she wrote in which she captured the feel of a small-town circus. The way she described the ring master allowed the reader to almost be there. Whenever she quoted him she put his words in all capital letters – not something she would normally do. But when he said, "LADIES AND GENTLEMEN, BOYS AND GIRLS," it was clear he was speaking to a small crowd and maybe dreaming he was at Madison Square Garden.

When Pat covered a bridge tournament, she encountered the kind of silence and stillness writers and photographers dread. How do you tell a story when there's no action? She solved it by imagining she was from another planet and had just dropped in to see what life was like on Earth. By changing her point of view, she was able to make the story come alive. Even the words the card players used appeared to be a secret, foreign language.

There are many time-tested ways of adding fun to your writing. Three great tools are the simile, the metaphor and personification.

When you use a simile, you're simply comparing something to something else. It usually requires you to use the words "like" or "as" or "similar to."

"It was like being in a crowded train station. The people were everywhere."

"She treated her Barbie dolls as if they were her own children."

"He never imagined there could be such a deep, yet barren canyon on a tropical island. It was similar to the Grand Canyon, but on a smaller scale."

When you use a metaphor, you are telling the reader that something is something else – even though it's not. The device allows you much more freedom. When you do it properly, the reader understands exactly what you're trying to say.

"The first day of college was a nightmare for Rudy. When he walked in the administration building, he encountered more people and confusion than he'd ever seen before. He was standing in Grand Central Station and everyone there was rushing to catch their train."

"The dolls were her children. She spoke to them and they spoke back to her."

"One minute he was on a tropical beach in Hawaii – and then, ten minutes later, he was standing in the middle of the Grand Canyon. He couldn't believe his eyes."

When you give human qualities to non-human things or animals, you're using the technique of personification. You can use it in just about every common writing application.

"The roots of the tree reached down more than 20 feet, grabbed the underground gas pipes and refused to let go."

"The Model T moaned as it struggled to make it up the steep hill."

"The church tower proudly looked down upon the rest of the buildings as it showed off its new bells."

"But the wedding dress sat alone in the closet, remembering its one day of glory and wishing it could somehow save Rhonda's failing marriage."

"The lonely highway meandered across the desert and

then climbed the mountain before it squeezed through the Cajon Pass. From there, it raced down the canyon to San Bernardino where it met up with the road from Blythe. They were both relieved they would not encounter any more of the desert heat."

While you're trying to have fun and be creative, you should avoid clichés like the plague. It's as easy as pie to get into a rut. Keep your eyes wide open, your hands on the wheel and your nose to the grindstone and you won't get caught with your pants down.

As you can see, it's easy to catch the cliché bug. You can have some fun, however, by taking one of those champions of overuse and change part of the sentence.

"I'll cross that marriage when I come to it."

"Where there's a will, there's a family."

"Don't change horses in the middle of the trial."

"Don't look a gift hamster in the mouth."

"It was an underwhelming experience."

"Once upon a timeshare."

"Until the twelfth of never mind."

"He was running around like a Republican with its head cut off."

"You can't tell a crook by its cover-up."

"It's a nice place to live, but I wouldn't want to visit there."

"I washed my hands and can't do a thing with them."

"Did you fall out of the wrong side of the bed this morning?"

Add some flavor to your writing by putting together words that begin with the same consonant or consonant sound. The technique is called alliteration.

"Kelly kept the closet clean and cleared of clutter."

"Fight for fitness, fight for fun or fight for freedom."

"Seven sailors sailed the seven seas for in seven seaworthy ships."

Sometimes you can select words that sound like the very action or thing you're writing about. You don't have to remember the term – onomatopoeia.

"The bull snorted and slobbered and grunted as the matador's cape swished past the animal's eyes."

"Fred's car zoomed past the entrance to the drive-in and then screeched to a stop."

"They looked into the gurgling volcano and gasped as it groaned and burped up vile gasses."

Exercise Number Five

Now it's time for you to write something using the techniques I've suggested. It could be a personal journal, a letter, an essay or a short story. You might want to take something you've already written and rework it into a piece of smooth writing.

Before you start, you may want to read the sample story that follows. Look at the verbs, the metaphors and the simple and compound sentences. Notice the absence of the passive voice. And notice that there's a theme running through it.

When you've completed your writing, have someone else read it aloud. If they can read it easily the first time through, you're probably doing well. If they stumble or have to go back and reread parts of it, you should do some more rewriting.

When you're satisfied with your writing, feel free to send me your story on e-mail. I'll do my best to critique it and e-mail it back to you. Please limit your samples to five or six pages. My e-mail address is donray@donray.com.

Happy writing.

Don Ray

Writing sample

Where it all comes together.

Read the published first-person essay below and look for examples of the writing tips you've learned:

Digging up the truth

An investigative reporter turns his skills on his own life, searching for answers about a man who tormented him for years.

By Don Ray

When I stepped off the plane I actually did kiss the ground. Then I headed home to surprise my folks. I had fibbed to them about the actual day I would return from Vietnam. First stop, Genio's Restaurant in Burbank. My Mom was the harried, lunch-time hostess returning from the back dining room – and I was just some impatient G.I. who wouldn't "Wait To Be Seated." She shook her head in frustration—she didn't really focus on my face until she got within about 15 feet of me. I think my marginal attempt at a mustache threw her off for an instant, but then she looked me in the eye. She gasped, she screamed and started running. She flung the menus she was carrying into the air and catapulted herself into my arms. It took the customers a beat or two to piece together what was happening—then they all stood up and applauded.

As memorable as that was, it would be my encounter with my stepfather that would remain in my mind as vividly as Jack Ruby shooting Lee Harvey Oswald. What I would learn that day would trouble me for the next 30 years.

"Surprise! I'm home!" He looked up at me from his recliner with those penetrating, grayish-blue eyes—eyes that had sent chills through me so many times in the decade he had been in our lives. He gave me that silent stare. I'm sure I sort of expected something akin to "welcome home," but instead he greeted me with one of those questions that was really his way of picking a fight.

"When are you going to cut off that goddamn mustache?" Now I was the one who was surprised—add to that incredulous and downright hurt. I tried not to react but he kept on poking at me with more cutting insults. It was when I asked him if I could use the car that he pushed me over the top. "Do you think you're grown up enough to borrow the car?" For the first time in my life I faced him off. You see, from the time he had married my mom when I was 10, he reigned as the undisputed power. I addressed him as "Sir"—or else. And he was always bigger enough that I wouldn't dare challenge him. Those eyes alone could make me buckle in fear. But not this time.

"I don't need this crap," I told him, in words a bit more graphic. "I've just spent a year dodging mortars and rockets and snipers' bullets and putting up with jungle rot, monster mosquitoes, cold showers and outdoor latrines. I've already been through hell and I'm not going to put up with it here." Zowie! For about three seconds I *was* the king. Then he not only dethroned me, he chopped my head off—at least his words did.

"You don't know what hell is," he said. Those eyes now seemed to cut right through me. "You don't know what it's like to follow some older idiots and end up in prison for fifteen years. Don't tell me about hell!"

Any details he provided were lost to the shocked daze I was now in. I seem to recall him saying something about teenagers knocking over a gas station, but I'm not sure. I am sure that I spent the next 30 years imagining what he must have gone through and how it might have accounted for the way he had treated me. It certainly could account for his two crooked fingers—maybe broken in prison and not properly set. It explained why he would never vote and why guns were taboo in our house And maybe I could even understand why he would become almost enraged if I blindly followed any group. And then there was his homophobia. It all seemed to make sense. In retrospect, I've always believed that I'd have been better off if he had told the truth from the start. Maybe I wouldn't have joined the Army and gone to Vietnam— just to get away from him.

We never talked about it again. He died five years later. Strangely, it's been in the 25 years since then I've felt the need to talk with him – to tap into his life experiences and his street wisdom. To tell him how angry he made me. A couple of times I've awakened in a sweat after being face-to-face with him in a troubling dream. I couldn't seem to escape those eyes.

It wasn't fair the way he treated me. And I'm sure it was my reaction to the that unfairness that eventually lead me to investigative journalism—a profession that empowers me to root out unfairness and injustice. How does it go, "Comfort the afflicted and afflict the comfortable?"

When I wasn't tracking down dirt on politicians and other shady characters, I would spend my free time using my skills to help people—anyone—to find their long-lost parents, friends and lovers. I think I was vicariously following an unconscious desire to find a father figure for myself. Over the years I've reunited enough people to fill a large bingo parlor.

But it was not until this year that I decided to steer my investigative skills in the direction of my own life. My mother recently passed away, so there was no real risk of hurting anyone by probing into my stepfather's past. A trusted psychologist cautioned me it could be overwhelming, but I knew I had to do it.

All I had known was his name, Edward C. Ripley, and his date of birth in 1910. I was pretty sure he was from Illinois. My mother was his second wife—or so I thought. Seems like I once saw a picture of a son from his first marriage, but my stepfather never spoke about him. It took a while, but I tracked down his prison file at the Illinois State Archives and had the archivist send me a copy of it: Edward C. Ripley, Inmate B-442.

It was a bit overwhelming. The first thing I saw was the mug shots of a 20-year-old kid in a coat and tie and little round spectacles. When I looked at his profile and I knew it was my stepfather. Then I looked at the full face and chills swept over my body. Those eyes were looking through me again. I had to catch my breath. Really. Then a strange realization hit me—we had done a reversal in ages. I was now the 50-year-old looking at the 20-year-old. And as I explored the file, I felt the urge to reach out to him—that I was the father figure he had needed.

With each page I turned I learned more shocking things about the man who had reared me. It wasn't a handful of teenagers at a gas station—it was three grown men and 19-year-old Edward C. Ripley pulling off what, today, we'd call a home invasion robbery, of a farmhouse in Evansville, IL. And it was my stepfather who tied up the couple, the grandparents and even the grandchildren and held a loaded revolver on them while the other men ransacked the house. They fled with $40,000 in negotiable bonds—a fortune in 1930 dollars.

And that wasn't all. Before this heist, he had embezzled $10,000 from a bank in St. Louis and was a suspect in at least one bank robbery. This was the guy who'd occasionally use his belt to paint red stripes on my bare backside—the guy who one time even punched me in the face and decked me when I came home late for dinner. Good thing I never seriously challenged him, I thought.

But there were also lots of details that somewhat mitigated his violence—the file chronicled his early life. He quit high school at age 15 and went to work at a bank so he could support his alcoholic, abusive father, his dying mother and two younger brothers. When the bank collapsed in 1929, he went to work at another bank—just long enough to steal the $10,000. It was while he was on the lam that he got involved with the robbers.

The file showed he served 11 years of hard time. They let him out on parole in September of 1941. At the time of his final release in 1945, the file had a most interesting entry: "He was divorced in 1944 and then married Pauline, his present wife. He has one son, David, age three years." Another marriage? Another son? I had to find him.

When I eventually made the call to Bismarck, ND, a man answered. "I'm looking for the David Peter Ripley who was born in Illinois to an Edward C. Ripley," I said. There was silence. He nervously cleared his throat. I could feel the electricity over the phone.

"Uh, yes, that's me," he said almost in the form of a question. I told him that I was pretty sure his father had brought me up and that he had passed away 25 years ago. David's voice quivered slightly as he said, "I've been looking for him for 50 years."

He had known about the prison time—his mother had told him the gas station story. And he knew his father had left them for another woman. He thought maybe he had a half brother. We talked for hours over the next couple of days and decided we had to find that boy from the second marriage. My sister agreed that his name was probably Dick and that maybe he had gone off to college at Texas A&M. The university confirmed that Richard Ray Ripley graduated back in the 1960s, and he last reported he was living in Port Lavaca, Texas. He, too, was listed.

He was equally shocked to hear from me. He had known about the previous marriage and the possible half brother, but he knew nothing about the prison time. I quickly put him in touch with David and they soon announced they were flying to Los Angeles to meet each other, my sister and me for the first time. It happened only weeks later.

When I looked at Richard, it was if I was looking at my stepfather. The same mouth, the same chin, the same nose, the same posture. But David had the eyes. He was smiling when we met, but those eyes could see right through me. At least that's what I thought. My sister and I felt compelled to study their every feature.

I had to conduct some training classes in Sacramento for state investigators—on how to find people—so the two brothers made the long drive with me. We had lots of time to get to know each other, share stories and coincidences. They sat in the back of the class as I told the story—ironically, to a room full of prison correction officers—of the most dramatic search of my life. The surprise was when I introduced them as my brothers. The entire class broke into applause. Many had tears in their eyes. I know I did.

It took three days for me to not flinch each time David looked at me with his father's eyes and to not get nervous when Richard would quietly take everything in the way my stepfather would. I was so nervous they felt compelled to remind me that they were not my stepfather. We dropped David off at a relative's house in San Francisco. He gave me the hug neither of us ever remember getting from Edward C. Ripley. We vowed to be brothers forever. All of a sudden those penetrating eyes took on a new meaning—they were now so loving and accepting. I wanted to study them more, but my own eyes were filling with tears.

Then Richard and I drove back to Burbank. Like his father, he didn't say much, but took everything in. When he spoke, it was words of wisdom—words of advice—words of encouragement. The next morning I took him to the airport. He waited till the very last minute to board. We hugged and patted and both avoided eye contact as he turned and walked away. I stood on the roof of the parking garage and watched his plane disappear into the haze. When I got home I looked again at the mug shots of Edward C.

Ripley. I can now see only the warm eyes and friendly faces of my two stepbrothers.

I've stopped looking for someone to be my father. And I tell people today not to mess with me "or my two older brothers will come here and kick your butt."